HOPE SPRINGS ETERNAL

2007–2019

ALEX TUTTLE

Hope Spring Eternal: 2007–2019

ISBN: 978-0-9989852-4-4

Published by Phase Eight Publishing,
an imprint of Phase Seven Comics.

http://www.phasesevencomics.com/phase8/

Edited by Alec Longstreth.

INTRODUCTION

I grew up playing on various sports teams with Alex Tuttle during the '90s in the suburbs of Seattle. I was never any good at baseball and spent most of my time languishing in the outfield or striking out at the plate. After limping along for a few years, I finally dropped the sport like a bad habit.

Alex on the other hand, loved baseball – still does! One entire wall of his childhood bedroom was a blown-up photographic mural of a packed baseball diamond, taken from the viewpoint of the center fielder. If memory serves, Alex played catcher. But besides his time on the little league diamond, it seemed like wherever we went in our adolescent years, Alex was always talking about baseball. Not only with our fellow students, but with parents, camp counselors, and teachers. He'd effortlessly rattle off statistics and the merits or weaknesses of individual players on the Mariners, which to my unschooled ear sounded like he was speaking a foreign language.

Annually, beginning in 2007, on the opening day of the Mariners' season, Alex sent out an email to his friends and family entitled "Hope Springs Eternal." At first these emails were full of inside jokes about current Mariners players and managers, which all went over my head. But just a couple of years into the project he began to meditate more generally on the

nature of hope. The stories strayed quite a bit from baseball –
World War II, Greek mythology, presidential races from half
a century ago, expeditions into the Amazon jungle – but he
always brought us back to the dugout in the end. I'll be damned
if Alex's waxing poetic about his beloved sport didn't make me
feel a little nostalgic for the national pastime, which, given my
background, was no small feat!

The first day of baseball is never circled on my calendar,
but now, more than a decade later, Alex's "Hope Spring
Eternal" email is the one I look forward to the most
each year. I think his writing is great, and I wanted
to share it with a wider audience by publishing this book.
I hope you'll enjoy it.

– Alec Longstreth, *Editor*
Phase Eight Publishing

For my uncle Bruce,
ever the optimist

2007

Yes, Mariner fans - It's that time of year again. Baseball is upon us. While certainly the Good Ship Mariner's destitute off-season has you looking down at your watches and waiting for the bitter end, there is reason for hope. Last year's 78-win campaign seems like ancient history doesn't it? Doesn't it?!?!?

Some old friends have moved on, sure. Instead of beginning opening day in the dugout rubbing moonshine on his aching, feminine shoulder, Gil Meche will be on a pitcher's mound in Kansas City, giving thousands of people a hopeful promise that will never be fulfilled. Instead of fine-tuning his swing in Safeco Field's underground batting cages as the first pitch draws nearer, Carl Everett will be aimlessly wandering around the Pacific Science Center's Dinosaur exhibit, wondering how it all went wrong. And instead of sitting on his laurels, watching his team take a pounding from the Oakland Athletics, Mike Hargrove will be.... wait, don't finish that thought.

In the first game of the 2007 season on Sunday night, the Mets defeated the Cardinals six to one. Between Jon Miller's cataclysmic pronunciation of the Hispanic players' names, and Joe Morgan repeating himself five times every half-inning - it appears that the 2007 season has picked up right where 2006 left off. And when the Mets wake up this morning, they will do so in first place, a half game ahead of the Nationals, Phillies, Braves, and the Florida team - all of whom are yet to play a game. The Cardinals, conversely, will be playing catchup to the Pirates, Reds, Brewers, Cubs, and Astros for the next 161 games. Yes, I can name all the teams.

But our precious Mariners needn't concern themselves with such details. Assuming Felix Hernandez gets a decent night's sleep and Hargrove doesn't set fire to his apartment complex, he will become the youngest opening day starter in Seattle team history. He will oppose Oakland's Dan Haren, who is the Athletics' almost as young, almost as filthy - but not quite - ace. On the line will be pride, honor, and first place in the AL West.

After lacing the Safeco Field Visitor's clubhouse water supply with cyanide this morning, I thought to myself, "Self, this could be a great summer. The Mariners could surprise everyone, including the eternally optimistic MacSlarrow of the north. Then again, Ichiro could slip on one of Mike Hargrove's drool puddles, break his ankle, and this could be the worst summer ever. Oh man, I love chocolate bunnies!"

So because we do it every spring, I'll just get right to the point: hope springs eternal.

For one day - for one brief, magical moment - everyone starts the season fresh. Zero and zero. If only everything just goes a little better this season than last.... if only those old grizzly veterans have one more season left in the tank.... if only Ichiro hits like it's 2004... if only King Felix can summon the strength from his elephant testicles and win 18 games.... if only Jeff

3

Weaver can hold the line at a 4.50 ERA... if only John McLaren could throw Mike Hargrove out of the team plane somewhere over the Rocky Mountains... If only.....

Because today everything can still go right. The division is still there for the taking. Today we are in first.

Do you think that on opening day last year, ANYONE believed the Tigers would go to the World Series? Or that anyone thought the 2001 Mariners would survive the loss of A-Rod? Or that Lou Piniella's 1990 Reds had a prayer? Hell no!

To quote Alexis de Tocqueville, that's why they play the games. Today, Mariner fans, everything can still go right.... For those of you who can make it, come to Pyramid brewery before the game (around 1) and drink - to hope. Even better, get a ticket, come to the center field beer garden, and drink - to King Felix. And throw empties at Mike Hargrove.

I know I will be. Because after a winter long, dark, and bereft of hope - at last it is time again.... to Play Ball!

Go M's!!

2007: 88 WINS / 74 LOSSES

2008

Good Morning Friends!

There is great beauty in the cycle of life. Throughout the year, there are constant reminders of just how lucky we truly are. The vitality of SUMMER frees us to explore the world and take in its beauty, and escape the dreary monotony of our daily charge. Each AUTUMN, we return home, gathering around the table with our friends and family to honor old traditions. The fond nostalgia of the past lines our memories like the fallen leaves line our streets. But just around the corner is the harsh reality of WINTER. When Chekhov saw the long winter, he saw a winter bleak and dark and bereft of hope. Yet we know that winter is just another step in the cycle of life.*

And then, one glorious day, we awake from our winter slumber. We step outside to see that the sun has replaced the clouds, light has taken the place of darkness, and the arrival of SPRING is not a moment too soon. That first breath of fresh spring air fills our lungs with childlike exuberance, freeing us from inhibition and restraint, giving us hope for the year ahead.

Some, in their old age, reject this optimism in favor of their own cynical reality. For these curmudgeons, the cycle of life is a prison, pinning them down in an endless circuit of predictability. Right now, you may be asking yourself, "Self, how can we bridge this divide between young and old, winter and spring, hope and cynicism?"† There is an answer.

I'm talking about baseball, friends.

The one constant through all the years has been baseball. America has rolled by like an army of steamrollers. It's been erased like a blackboard, rebuilt, and erased again, but baseball has marked the time. This field, this game, it's a part of our past.... It reminds us of all that once was good, and could be again.^

The national pastime is intertwined with every step of our country's great history. In fact, the chosen game of the colonists during the War of British Aggression was the seed that sprouted into the modern baseball we enjoy today. During the Civil War, the Blues and Grays put aside their differences long enough to play nine innings between battles. And when our 27th President stood up in the 7th inning and started the stretch, it wasn't to see a Hydroplane jump a floating Oberto! ramp or to start "The Wave," it was to smell the fresh frankfurters, take in the afternoon breeze, and live the American dream.[a] And on one fateful April 15th in 1947, when most Americans were filing their taxes with Uncle Sam, Jackie Robinson was breaking the nation's oppressive color barrier. And for my money, there's nothing more American than baseball, taxes, and pretending not to be racist.

Yes, friends, baseball has marked the time.... And for six long, excruciating years, our beloved Mariners have lagged behind their division rivals. We've watched, in horror, as evil disease-ridden Anaheim Rally Monkeys have celebrated in Safeco Field on OUR scientifically engineered Kentucky bluegrass!! Finally, the time has come to send them a message. It is time to say, once and for all:

NOT THIS YEAR HALOS! GO BACK TO YOUR PLASTIC

DISNEY BUNKER OF EVIL AND YOUR DIRTY FRIENDS!

Today, Mariner fans, we begin a prodigious journey. It is still only spring, but already I can see King Felix laying claim to his throne, Ichiro painting the outfield with his singles, and Yuniesky gliding into the hole and gobbling up everything within reach. But Mariner fans, it is not they who will carry us to October.

Our fate rests on the shoulders of a southpaw from Ottawa. He is Erik, son of Bedard. Will he buckle the knees of American League hitters with his mighty curveball? Will he penetrate the teste satchel of the evil empire to the south? Will he be the ace that's been missing since Chuck Armstrong showed Randy Johnson the door to Houston? Or will he follow in the shallow footsteps of Kevin Mitchell and Heathcliff Slocumb, and merely tease us with expectations?

The answer, my friends, lies in the summer ahead. Our path is uncharted, our dreams are within reach. October, like the cold winter, is just around the corner.

But today, hope springs eternal.

Play Ball!!

Bibliography
* Phil Connors, Groundhog Day (1993).
† You may also be asking, "why are you citing to yourself?" Just have another chocolate bunny.
^ Terry Mann, Field of Dreams (1989).
ª William H. Taft LOVED frankfurters. Loved, loved, loved.

2008: 61 WINS / 101 LOSSES

2009

Friends,

In the winter of 1943, it appeared to many in occupied France that the evil reign of tyranny would never end. Nazi oppression became more brutal by the day. The French people patiently stood by, waiting for the Allies to liberate their people, but three years of waiting, for some, was just too long. The curfew and food rations became more and more strict as the Nazis tightened their iron grip on Europe. Some took their own lives. Everyone suffered.

But quietly, a small yet potent resistance movement sprouted. Despite tremendous risk, this band of brave citizens began to organize, giving food and shelter to their allies, tracking enemy troop positions, and providing invaluable assistance to the Allied forces. Those who were detected paid the ultimate price, but what choice did they have? Without hope, they had nothing.

By the spring of 1944, as the flowers began to blossom, "La Résistance" had amassed more than 100,000 members. Among them were children who delivered vital documents via their bicycles, women who smuggled weapons to one another in innocuous baskets of clothing and food, and men who gathered late at night, risking life and limb in violation of the dreaded curfew.

Finally, on June 6, 1944, the wait was over. On that day, 160,000 Allied troops landed on the beaches of Normandy, driving the Nazi forces back. Eventually three million Allied soldiers stormed across that beachhead, driving the Nazis back across the Seine River by summer's end. On August 25th, the French flag was flying over Paris for the first time since the war began. France was free again.

This spring I am reminded of that fateful summer as it pertains to our beloved Seattle Mariners. Much like the French military, we Mariner fans have had very little to cheer about over the years. After thirty-two long and pitiful seasons, we begin another spring with nothing but a mere hope of attaining that elusive World Series banner.

But still.... there is always hope.

Sixty-four years after the liberation of France, Mariner fans were also freed from the tyranny of their oppressor. On June 16, 2008, Bill Bavasi was terminated as GM, after a long and destructive reign over baseball operations. The resistance movement – phone calls to sports-radio, bitter letters to the editor, persistent booing – finally drove out the enemy. We were free again!!

Just as the cold winter twists the knife with its harshness, there always comes a single day when that first ray of light shines down upon your shoulders. One glorious morning, we awake from our winter slumber and step outside to see that the sun has replaced the clouds and that light has taken the place of darkness. That first breath of fresh spring air fills our lungs with strength, ready to be unleashed in the coming days, giving us hope for the year ahead.

This may not be the year our beloved Mariners finally float down Fourth Avenue in their victory parade, but many champions have been accidental. The Miracle Mets didn't know when they lost on Opening Day 1969 that they would eventually be the last men standing. The St. Louis Cardinals of 2006 didn't know on Opening Day that 83 wins and one Jeff Weaver later, they would be the champions. And the French resisters that filled the streets of Paris in the spring of 1944 didn't know if their liberators would ever cross the English channel. But all raised the flag of victory.

Everything can change in a day. And on this day, we all start anew. It's Opening Day, my friends! And hope springs eternal.

Let's play ball!!

2009: 85 WINS / 77 LOSSES

2010

Good Morning.

Just over forty-two years ago today, at the peak of the war in Vietnam, a relentless American bombing campaign virtually destroyed the Vietnamese city of Ben Tre and killed a number of civilians. An American Major explained the tragedy to a reporter by insisting that, "we had to destroy the village in order to save it." That quote eventually became a rallying cry for opponents of the war, and it helped sway public opinion against the violence in Southeast Asia.

Four decades later, across the Pacific Ocean, another local institution went up in flames. Of course, I'm talking about the Seattle Mariners, and their torch-bearer Bill Bavasi. With Bavasi in charge, the Good Ship Mariner was lost at sea for four long years, while our once-proud baseball franchise became a national laughingstock. Mariner fans everywhere openly wondered when (and if) the torment would ever end.

But the village had to be destroyed before it could be saved.

Just south of Ben Tre's remains, in the heart of the Mekong Delta, there lies a refuge called "Phoenix Island." During the tumultuous 1960s, an inspirational Zen Master known as the "The Coconut Monk" developed a spiritual haven on the island that came to be recognized as a place of peace and hope, and a symbol of the virtue that can emerge even in spite of a brutal war.

Closer to home, another Phoenix Island can be found rising above the offices overlooking Edgar Martinez Drive. Its caretaker is the inspirational Ninja in a Sweater Vest, Jack Zduriencik, whose shrewd transactions have given us hope and allowed us to forget the abysmal Bavasi era. Despite inheriting a miserable farm system and an aging player roster, Zduriencik has transformed the Mariners into contenders again in just over one year on the job.

The pennant race is on.

There are no guarantees in life, friends. In the long, rich history of America's pastime, even commanding leads have been squandered at the hands of improbable dark horses. But this summer, after nearly a decade in the shadows, the pennant race returns to Seattle. With two aces leading the way, will 2010 finally be the year that the Good Ship Mariner sails down Fourth Avenue in a victory parade?

Hope springs eternal.

I know it wasn't long ago that our village was burned to the ground, Mariner fans. Each grueling defeat tested our will, crushed our spirit, and exhausted our hope. But we must not surrender! We must rebuild! Tonight, when King Felix Hernandez steps onto the mound in Oakland, it will be the first pitch of the 2010 American League West pennant race. At that moment, friends, do me this favor: close your eyes and imagine....

October.

Play Ball!

2010: 61 WINS / 101 LOSSES

Good Morning Friends!

On a morning like this, it's hard not to cherish the pioneers who pushed the limits of human discovery.

Around the turn of the twentieth century, Percy Fawcett, an unassuming Englishman with a thirst for adventure, resigned his commission from the British Army and joined the Royal Geographic Society to map uncharted territories in the Americas. In 1906, Fawcett was dispatched to the Amazon to survey the border territory between Brazil and Bolivia. It was a dangerous jungle that only the bravest of souls dared to enter.

The jungle was dark, perpetually damp, and disease-ridden insects swarmed through the air as thick as smoke. There were legions of dangerous, wild animals and edible food was scarce. For many explorers of the era, the Amazon was a suicide mission. Many of Fawcett's peers were afflicted with gangrene or malaria. Some even died. However, somewhat bizarrely, Fawcett fell in love with the mighty jungle. He made seven long expeditions into the Amazon for the RGS between 1906 and 1924. He knew the terrain and local culture as well as any foreigner.

But the jungle was about more than mere exploration to Fawcett. By 1917, he had come to believe that there was a lost city buried deep within the Amazon. As he uncovered each new clue, he became obsessed with finding the ancient ruins. He tirelessly researched ancient texts, furiously scribbled in his notebook, and even wrote in secret code to conceal his notes from competing explorers. Fawcett's family became estranged from him. When he was at home in England between expeditions, he would become depressed. He longed to return to the mighty jungle and dreamed of nothing but discovering its ancient jewel.

Finally, in April of 1925, Fawcett cobbled together enough funding to embark on what would be his final journey. With only his eldest son and one other companion at his side, Fawcett set out into the heart of the jungle to find the lost city once and for all....

He was never heard from again.

Percy Fawcett died in pursuit of a dream. He combatted disease, unruly wildlife, hostile tribes, and little or no food for weeks at a time, all in the name of discovery.

Friends, we share something in common with the great Fawcett. We too are searching for our lost city. We have patiently waited for an American League pennant since 1977. We have passionately supported our beloved Seattle Mariners Baseball Club through thick and thin. And we have suffered through countless agonizing defeats for the last three and a half decades.

But on this day, hope springs eternal.

Dare to dream today, Mariner fans. Spring is here, the birds are chirping, and the fresh, warm air fills us with vitality on every breath. Who's to say that 2011 won't end in a victory parade? After several miserable seasons of rebuilding, our Mariners have finally devoted their attention to building a contender from within. Young stars like Justin Smoak, Dustin Ackley, and Michael Pineda are on their way to join King Felix in Seattle. The Good Ship Mariner has plotted a new course.

Today, we set sail for victory!

Percy Fawcett looked outside his dreary English bungalow and dreamed about what was possible. He devoted his life to discovering something unique and unforgettable, enduring brutally harsh conditions just so he could share it with the world. Our Mariners, much like Fawcett, might very well be marching into certain death. But the search for the elusive pennant must go on.

Happy Opening Day

Let's play ball!

2011: 67 WINS / 95 LOSSES

2012

Good Morning Friends!

In perhaps his most famous literary work, Samuel Coleridge wrote of an Ancient Mariner, tanned but weathered from his days at sea. The Mariner is sitting outside a lively wedding reception, where inside a young couple is celebrating their eternal love. The Mariner spots a young party guest on his way to join in the celebration. The Mariner pulls aside this young man and begins to share his tales of woe on the high seas, and the young man listens attentively as the party goes on behind them.

Once in his younger days, the Ancient Mariner recalls, a large storm forced his ship into an icy patch of ocean. The crew was in grave danger, they did not think they would survive. At that moment, a mighty albatross appeared overhead. As the bird flew above the ship, the icy waters began to break up, opening up a path for the sailors to escape the treacherous waters. Wherever the bird flew, a calm breeze and cool mist followed in its wake, guiding the ship to safety. The men followed this bird for many days, believing it to be their savior.

But one day, on impulse, the Ancient Mariner shot and killed the albatross by mistake.

The gentle breeze subsided. The cool mist turned into a blistering sun. And the men were stranded on a stagnant boat awaiting a gust of wind to carry them home. The drinkable water was long gone. After several days in these brutal conditions, the men's throats were so dry that they could not even speak to one another. The other men were so angry at the Mariner that they hung the albatross around his neck as a reminder of what he had done.

After several days, a ship appeared on the horizon. The men were too fatigued and their throats too dry to call for aid. So the Mariner bit into his own arm, sucked out just enough blood to moisten his throat, and called out to the sailors across the horizon. He screamed for hours, but the ship was merely an empty vessel drifting on the open sea. It was all a mirage.

Slowly the other men began to die, leaving only the Ancient Mariner with the albatross hanging around his neck. As he fell asleep each night he dreamed of the other men, taunting and berating him for the death of the albatross that led to their demise. He was haunted by their images and ridden with guilt for many nights.

Drinking only rainwater, the Mariner eventually drifted back to his native soil, barely clinging to life. There he was spotted by an old hermit who, along with another man, deployed a rescue boat to retrieve him. The Mariner was so gaunt and lifeless that the rescuers believed him to be dead. But just as they carried him into the lifeboat, the Mariner awoke, lamenting his existence and grieving over the loss of his fellow sailors. He told his rescuers every word of his woeful story, each detail more agonizing than the next.

As he told his tale, however, the Mariner noticed that he began to feel much better. As time went on, the Mariner came to realize that he has been cursed by the once powerful albatross. Whenever he has not told his story for some time, it builds up inside him, making him sick to his stomach. He must then tell his story to whoever will listen to relieve himself of the agony.

As the young wedding guest listened intently to the Ancient Mariner, he is so stunned and distraught by his tale that he turns around and heads home, forgetting all about the joyous wedding party to which he had intended to go. He woke up the next morning feeling sadder, but wiser for having heard the Ancient Mariner's tale.

Samuel Coleridge died in 1834. But The Curse of the Ancient Mariner lives on....

Each spring, we are reminded of hope and possibility. That first breath of fresh spring air, that first ray of warm sun glancing across the nape of our necks, that first morning song from a neighboring swallow – together they mark a new beginning in the cycle of life. Leaves return to the trees. Rain clouds give way to sunshine. And the Seattle Mariners begin a new season, the American League pennant within their reach.

Coleridge's Rime of the Ancient Mariner serves to remind us that no matter how bad things may seem, no matter how desperate we are, no matter how much it feels like a curse has befallen each one of us: pain is only temporary, hope is forever.

Share your tale of woe, friends. Give others the wisdom they cannot give to themselves. There is only one team that has never won the American League pennant, and it's your Seattle Mariners. The albatross hanging around our necks, the oppressive ownership led by Howard Lincoln and Nintendo, is constantly creating obstacles in our path. They can publicly oppose a new arena in Seattle, they can cut payroll for the fourth consecutive year, and they can even raise ticket and concession prices in the midst of a stagnant economy.

But there is one place in which these greedy owners cannot go, and it is on the diamond.

There, between the white chalk, amidst the lush Kentucky Bluegrass, where the games are played to the busy hum of the crowd and the sharp crack of the bat, is where our fate is truly decided. And today, the Mariners sit on top of the AL West, ready to make a run at that elusive pennant once more.

Happy Opening Day!

Today, for one brief moment, we are free to believe that this could be the year. We can dismiss our limitations and embrace the possibilities of the coming season. We can close our eyes and imagine a victory parade. Today, we can put aside our differences and come together for one common goal.

Today.... Hope Springs Eternal.

2012: 75 WINS / 87 LOSSES

2013

Good Morning Friends!

On this beautiful spring morning, I am reminded of a story that my grandfather told me many years ago....

Hsiang Yu and Liu Pang were ambitious generals in the Chinese military who ascended through the ranks as friends and allies. But there was a crucial difference between them: Hsiang Yu descended from aristocracy, while Liu Pang was a peasant who had risen to his powerful position with nothing more than cunning and guile.

Around 208 BC, the King of Ch'u dispatched the two generals to dispose of a rival leader. Hsiang Yu was instructed to go north under the command of another general, while Liu Pang was to lead a direct attack. Hsiang Yu could not bear the thought of his peasant colleague reaching the target first and winning control of all the northern armies. When his commanding officer ordered troops to wait at the edge of the target city, Hsiang Yu grew so frustrated with his commander's lack of urgency that he beheaded his superior and assumed control of the northern attack.

But it was too late; Liu Pang's smaller, swifter army reached the enemy first. But this did not stop the ruthless Hsiang Yu. He chased Liu Pang from city to city, finally pinning him down in a secluded mountain town. For several days, Liu Pang hunkered down, refusing to surrender to his rival, believing that doing so would spell certain death for him and his men. But rather than just going in for the kill, Hsiang Yu waited his rival out, a costly mistake that eventually allowed Liu Pang to escape at a vulnerable moment. In the end, the ruthless general didn't have the stomach to destroy the man he once considered a friend.

Some time later, while Hsiang Yu's army was on sabbatical and dispersed across the northern territories, the elusive Liu Pang launched an unexpected attack, surrounding Hsiang Yu's primary garrison. Hsiang Yu's mercy had been rewarded with a humiliating defeat. Rather than surrender to a man whom he saw as a lowly peasant, the decorated Hsiang Yu cut his own throat in shame. Liu Pang used the death of his rival to consolidate the northern forces and, years later, became Emperor and launched the Han dynasty.

I am reminded of this story, my friends, because we share something in common with the immortal Liu Pang, who had his back against the wall with nothing left...

Except hope.

It is not the challenges we face that define us, but the courage that they inspire. All that stood between Liu Pang and death was the mercy of one man. Hsiang Yu's fatal mistake was that he did not crush his enemy when he had the chance. Rather than achieve total victory, he let his wily rival escape with a sliver of hope. Without which, he would not have had the courage to refuse to surrender and plot his escape. He would not have had the temerity to fight back despite being outnumbered. He would never have become Emperor.

It all begins with hope...

Each spring, as we feel that first warm ray of sunshine graze the nape of our necks, and we finally cast aside the ennui of winter, we are given the gift of hope. One glorious morning, we awaken from our winter slumber and step outside to see that the sun has replaced the clouds and that light has taken the place of darkness. That first breath of fresh spring air fills our lungs with exuberance and vitality and gives us the strength to confront life's biggest challenges.

If you are a Mariners fan, you have looked death in the face. And yet on this beautiful spring morning, on the doorstep of possibility, hope flutters through the air like the songs of a nearby swallow. Take this opportunity to close your eyes and imagine what the future may hold. There will be many rainy days on the horizon, my friends, just as there is always time to lament the past.

But on this Opening Day, as the Mariners step into the batters box for the first time, close your eyes and dream about a cool October night with red, white & blue bunting hanging from the steel rafters of Safeco Field. Dream about Felix Hernandez throwing his fists in the air as his teammates come running out of the first base dugout. Dream about the victory parade rolling down Second Avenue. Just dream.

Because on this day:

Hope springs eternal.

2013: 71 WINS / 91 LOSSES

2014

Good Morning Friends!

I find it heartening to look outside on this beautiful spring morning and see the sun penetrating the sky's usual gloomy, gray shield. In many ways, the first day of spring is the true beginning of the new year, giving us all a sense of optimism about the future that lies ahead. But those sixteenth century Catholics really wanted to move Easter to boost second quarter earnings, so we're stuck with the flawed Gregorian calendar. But I digress...

Nothing lifts my spirits like sunshine on Opening Day. In the Pacific Northwest, when the sun finally emerges after a long winter slumber, it illuminates the beauty of our region and injects energy and vitality into its people. And on this Opening Day, I need all the vitality I can get. For ten long years on this day, as I've written to many of you, the summers have been getting shorter and shorter for the hometown nine. Every year at about this time, I close my eyes and yearn for the electricity of October baseball that continues to elude our city. And every year the day that I am forced to face the cold reality of defeat comes earlier.

Today, as we get ready to embark on yet another attempt by the Seattle Mariners to crack the glass ceiling of the American League West, I am reminded of the timeless Myth of Sisyphus.

24

King Sisyphus was a conniving, avaricious figure in ancient Greek mythology. He took pleasure in killing his rivals, deceiving them, and even resorted to seducing their family members when it suited his interests. After one such transgression, the Gods ordered Sisyphus to be chained and imprisoned in the underworld until his death. But the clever Sisyphus tricked his captor into shackling himself and escaped yet again. Furious that they could not kill him, the Gods sentenced Sisyphus to one final punishment: they condemned him to pushing a large boulder up a mountain, only to watch it roll down once it reached the top. This futile task, which he was forced to repeat for eternity, was designed to be so cruel that Sisyphus would wish he was dead.

On this Opening Day, it's hard not to sympathize with the crestfallen Sisyphus walking down the mountain to retrieve the fallen boulder. Even if he was a philandering murderer.

After all, it would certainly come as a colossal surprise if the Good Ship Mariner was still sailing in October's playoffs. But as Kurt Vonnegut once wrote, "History is merely a list of surprises." Did anyone think two weeks ago that Connecticut would be going to the Final Four? Did anyone expect the American victory over the mighty British military at Yorktown?

As the saying goes, that's why they play the games.

Albert Camus, the renowned French philosopher, has studied and written extensively about the Myth of Sisyphus. Camus concludes that once Sisyphus finally acknowledges the futility of his task and the certainty of his fate, he is freed to realize the absurdity of his situation and reach a state of contented acceptance. Indeed, he wrote, "...one must imagine Sisyphus happy."

On this Opening Day, my friends, I too am happy. I still thirst for another taste of what George Will calls "the cruel addiction" of baseball.

I have descended the mountain again; the boulder is resting at my feet. And as I look up and consider the task ahead, I cannot help but feel a sense of contentment. Another magnificent northwest summer lies on our doorstep. For the next one hundred eighty days, the boys of summer will storm out of the dugout and onto the lush Kentucky bluegrass, taking the field with the best in the world in an iconic ballpark nestled up against Puget Sound. I will breathe in the fresh, Pacific marine air and bask in Seattle's idyllic weather with a cool northwest ale in my hand. And I will look up from my perch on Lookout Landing and watch the gorgeous sunsets over the Olympic Mountains.

But as I start up the mountain on this beautiful morning in the Emerald City, I am reminded that the severity of Sisyphus' punishment was not the task itself but its term: eternity. And although the road is steep and the boulder is heavy, the hapless Sisyphus and I are not the same. Because I will always draw from the one abiding belief that drives me up the mountain...

Hope springs eternal.

2014: 87 WINS / 75 LOSSES

2015

Good Morning Friends!

On this beautiful spring morning, when you step outside and see the sun glistening in the corner of your eye and you smell the scent of fresh flowers breezing across your face, take a moment to harken back to the gloomy winter that has hovered over our city for the last fourteen years.

You may remember the glorious summer of 2001 like I do. I was twenty-one years old, living on my own, finishing up college, and – regrettably – wearing tapered jeans. When the fashion police weren't hot on my trail that summer, you could usually find me sitting in the shirtsleeves at the ballpark on Royal Brougham Way, sipping a cold northwest ale, and listening to the Burlington Northern whistle by. Life doesn't get much better than a warm summer night at Safeco Field. Yet even by those lofty standards, the summer of 2001 was one for the ages. With Sweet Lou Piniella at the helm, our beloved Mariners set a baseball record for most wins in a season. You couldn't walk into a gas station that summer without the cashier asking whether the hometown nine had won (again!?) the night before.

Little did we know, winter was coming.

I can't help but think of all those dark winter days we've endured over the last fourteen years. Days when I truly believed that all hope was lost. I've compared our beloved baseball team to Sisyphus interminably pushing his boulder up the mountain. To explorers marching into certain death in the Amazon jungle. War. Murder. Tragedy. I honestly wondered if I would eventually disintegrate into an old codger, bouncing his grandchildren on his knee and boring them with stories of all the heartbreaking losses over the years, lamenting the fact that the Boys of Summer never brought the trophy home.

Friends, it has been a long winter: cold, dark, and bereft of hope. But today spring is on our doorstep.

History is littered with examples of long waits. You may remember when, back in 1906, a man named Harland Sanders falsified his own birth certificate to join the army at the age of 16. After being discharged, he caught on with the railroads. He worked as a blacksmith, then as a day laborer. At one point he became a firefighter. At night he studied law, and although he eventually became a lawyer, he was disbarred soon thereafter for assaulting his own client. [If you're going to get disbarred, you might as well go down swinging.] In all, he was fired from a dozen different jobs until he finally settled into operating a service station in Corbin, Kentucky in the 1930s. He became known for cooking warm meals for weary travelers and eventually he opened his own restaurant. But it was destroyed by a fire in 1939. In 1952, his reopened restaurant went belly-up when Interstate 75 redirected the route of travel. In 1955, at age 65, "Colonel" Harland Sanders didn't have a penny to his name. He cashed his first Social Security check and most people probably expected him to live out his days in destitute retirement.

But he never lost hope...

He believed in himself and his recipe too much, and he shocked his friends and family by using the money to open one last restaurant. After decades of failure and a vagabond's luck, Harland Sanders finally tasted the sweet nectar of victory. By 1964, Kentucky Fried Chicken had 600 locations worldwide and the colonel with the smug look on his face was a millionaire and a household name. Just when everyone had given up on Harland Sanders, when by all accounts he should have given up on himself, he took one Social Security check and turned it into a fast food empire. And probably, heart disease.

It has been a long, harsh winter, Mariners fans. Your patience has been tested. Your optimism has been shattered. You've paid escalating ticket prices to watch a hapless collection of goons toss the ball around the diamond for far too long. But this season, there just might be joy in Mudville once again...

As I step outside today into the fresh, northwest spring air, I will remember the long, grueling winter that was. I will think of Dave Niehaus, the smooth velvet voice of summer. I will think of The Kid climbing the fence to take away another home run. But mostly I will think of that bright-eyed, bushy-tailed twenty-one year old boy who sat out in the bleachers with the sun shining down on him, a scorebook in his hand, who didn't have a care in the world. He was glued to every pitch, believing that his Mariners would one day raise a banner above the

Emerald City. The last fourteen years have taken their toll on the boy. His bright eyes have grown cynical. His bushy tail has a few gray hairs.

But maybe this summer he can be a boy again.

Hope springs eternal.

2015: 76 WINS / 86 LOSSES

2016

Good Morning Friends!

In the gloomy Pacific Northwest, winter can be onerous. When the calendar turns to spring, the sunshine is not only a welcome change, it is the symbol of hope for a new year. That first warm ray of sunlight each spring is a sign that the glorious Seattle summer is right around the corner. And so is the return of the hometown nine. All across America today, fans like you and I will open our newspapers and see our beloved baseball team sitting at the top of the standings, next to the east coast elites and the midwest juggernauts. We may harbor some doubts about this year's squad, but for one day at least, the World Series that continues to elude the Emerald City appears within our grasp.

If you aren't brimming with hope on this fine spring morning, then let me remind you that history is littered with examples of underdogs that prevailed against all odds. During this dramatic and unpredictable political season, I am reminded of one particularly poignant example; it was perhaps the most stunning turn of events in American electoral history.

After suffering four consecutive defeats in Presidential elections, Republicans met in Philadelphia for their convention on June 21, 1948. Without the iconic Democrat Franklin Delano Roosevelt at the top of the ticket, Republicans believed that their nominee would be a heavy favorite to defeat the incumbent President Harry Truman, who had serendipitously ascended to the Oval Office after FDR's death.

Republican senators Robert Taft and Arthur Vandenberg, and governors Harold Stassen and Earl Warren all vied for the nomination, trying to stop the one Republican who had come closer than anyone to defeating FDR: New York governor Thomas Dewey. Dewey was known for his controversial opinions, such as his theory that FDR knew about the attack on Pearl Harbor. But because the anti-Dewey forces failed to consolidate around one candidate, the "Stop Dewey" movement failed, and the New York governor won the closely contested nomination on the third ballot.

Nevertheless, Dewey began the summer as a heavy favorite. Truman had struggled to lead the nation smoothly through its transition out of World War II and into a peacetime economy. A railroad strike, heavy inflation, and a controversial decision to integrate the Armed Forces had taken their toll on his favorability. The Republicans had assumed control of

Congress in the 1946 midterm elections, enabling the GOP to finally halt the growth of government that had symbolized the New Deal. Truman's approval was measured as low as 36% with the election approaching.

To make matters worse, Truman's unorthodox positions had caused a split in the Democratic Party. Truman's predecessor as FDR's Vice President, Henry Wallace, led the Progressive Party, which railed against Truman for allowing large corporations to rig the economy! The Dixiecrat Party consolidated in the South to oppose Truman's advocacy on civil rights. By mid-summer, no one outside of Truman's hometown of Independence, Missouri thought he had a snowball's chance of hanging on to the White House in November.

But the Republicans overplayed their hand.

The 80th Congress went to such lengths to oppose Truman's agenda that Truman labeled it the "Do Nothing Congress." He made Republican obstruction a major issue in the general election, barnstorming across the country on his famous "Whistle-stop Tour." He traveled from state to state, making his case directly to the voters. But without frequent public opinion polls to track his progress, the nation was so convinced that Dewey would win that nearly every major media outlet projected him as the winner on the night of the election.

You'll never believe what happened next....

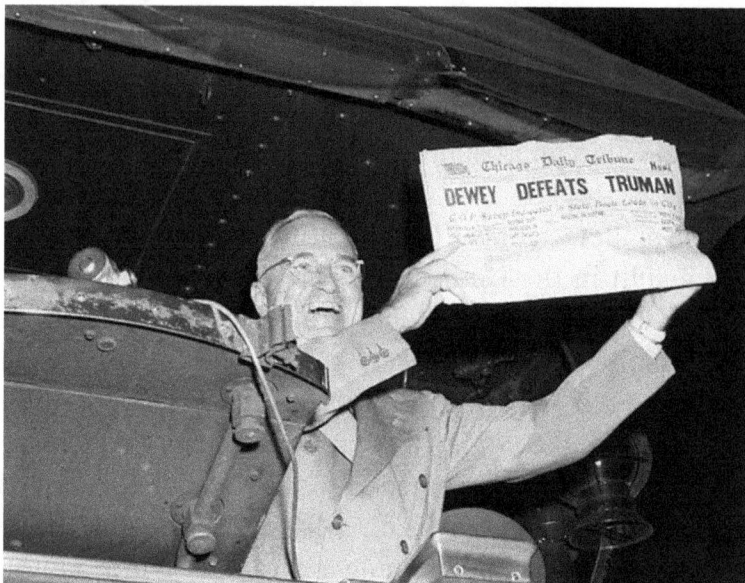

Harry S. Truman, the accidental 33rd President of the United States, overcame insurmountable odds to overwhelmingly win reelection on November 2, 1948. He prevailed when everyone from the Everglades to the Cascades thought he was dead in the water.

He never lost hope.

Let the 1948 election serve as an important reminder that no odds are insurmountable, even in these turbulent times. The Seattle Mariners begin the 2016 season today in first place. The American League West is there for the taking. This is our day to dream. To imagine what's possible, not merely likely.

When Harry Truman embarked on the Whistle-stop tour in the summer of 1948, no one gave him a chance. His adversaries sat on their duffs in their fancy hotel rooms and drank their fancy boxed wine and waited for the votes to roll in while Truman shook every hand and kissed every baby from Dubuque to DC. That's why they play the games.

Someday, baseball fans, we will have the last laugh. We will sneak up on everyone and bring the World Series trophy home to Seattle. We will watch as the glorious victory parade rolls down Fourth Avenue. We will watch King Felix and some guy named Scott Servais wave to the crowd as the blue and teal confetti trickles down to the ground below them. We will remember all those gloomy winter mornings when we never thought we'd live to see the Mariners win it all. And when we do, we will remember this day.... where it all started.

Hope springs eternal.

2016: 86 WINS / 76 LOSSES

2017

Happy Opening Day!

It occurs to me that after all the poignant historical analogies and obscure tales I've told in this space over the years, it's easy to forget what brought us together in the first place: the national pastime itself.

Baseball was my first love. When I wasn't playing catch with the old man deep into the summer twilight or catching pop-ups on the playground with my classmates, I was looking for baseball anywhere I could find it. I can remember watching all nine telecasts of Ken Burns' Baseball as they aired live on PBS. (Wither the NEA!) And listening to the dulcet tones of Dave Niehaus reading "Casey at the Bat" on my old faux-wood-panel clock radio after a game. But what most of you may not know is that loving baseball taught me to love reading. Baseball was the one subject I couldn't get enough of. I devoured *The Boys of Summer* by Roger Kahn, about the great Brooklyn Dodgers teams that led fans to coin the famous phrase, "Wait 'till next year." And *Shoeless Joe* by W.P. Kinsella, the novel that inspired *Field of Dreams*. *Men at Work* by George Will, the timeless treatise about the craft of baseball, is one of my favorites. I read them all and many more.

But every year about this time, there is one story that always comes to mind: *Summer of '49* by David Halberstam.

When the great ballplayers returned home from World War II,

the so-called "Golden Age" of baseball shifted into high gear. The New York Yankees, led by Hall of Famers Joe DiMaggio, Yogi Berra, Johnny Mize, and Phil Rizzuto won fifteen American League pennants between 1946 and 1964. Their chief rival in the American League was, as it has always been, the Boston Red Sox, led by the great Ted Williams, fan favorite Bobby Doerr, and Joe's brother, Dom DiMaggio. And don't forget about the Cleveland Indians, the only other team to win an AL pennant during that time. The Indians had seven Hall of Famers of their own, including Bob Feller, Satchel Paige, Bob Lemon, and Larry Doby. The pride of the National League were those Boys of Summer from Brooklyn, led by Duke Snider, Jackie Robinson, Roy Campanella, and Pee Wee Reese.

Back then a young boy could scrape together a couple dimes, hop the train, sneak under the turnstiles, walk into one of the old cathedrals of the game, watch a dozen Hall of Famers, and still be home for dinner. ESPN wasn't there to replay the relief pitcher putting bubble gum on his teammate's hat in between ads for Coors Light. Fans read the newspaper and listened to their favorite radio announcers describe the action. If a kid wanted to actually see the hometown nine, he had to cut school and hitch a ride to the ballpark. And when he got there, he didn't watch blooper reels and play music trivia in between innings. (Maybe organ music trivia?) The descriptions of the game authored by the era's great sportswriters – the crack of the bat, the snap the fastball makes in the palm of the catcher's glove, the buzz of the crowd after a close slide into third – made the game come alive for the many fans that only wished they could have been there. It's called the Golden Age for a reason, folks.

The Summer of '49 was one of the great pennant races of all time. Throughout the summer, the Yankees led the American League standings, but were followed closely by the Red Sox and the Indians. The Dodgers and the Cardinals dueled atop the National League. But as the calendar flipped to September, Cleveland began to fade. The Indians lost eleven games between September 8 and September 24, slipping out of the race. Then, on September 18, misfortune struck the Bronx when Joe DiMaggio, the heart and soul of the Yankees (if Yankees have souls), came down with pneumonia.

Over the next two weeks without DiMaggio in the lineup, the Yankees went just 6-6 and the Yankee Clipper lost 18 pounds battling the illness. On September 26, after trailing the Yankees all summer (by as many as 11 games on July 5), the Red Sox moved into first place with a three-game sweep of their arch rivals at Fenway Park. In the National League, the Dodgers swept a doubleheader on September 29 to take a one-half game lead over the Cardinals. The race in the NL was never larger than four games.

On Saturday October 1, Boston clung to a one-game lead over New York with just two to play. As the arch rivals returned to the Big Apple, the Yankees had no margin for error. The Red Sox needed to win just one game to clinch the pennant. That afternoon, after two excruciating weeks, Joltin' Joe DiMaggio returned to the Yankee lineup. In the fourth inning, with his team trailing 4-0 and facing elimination, DiMaggio laced a double into the gap, igniting a rally that led the Yankees to a 5-4 victory. Meanwhile, with the Cardinals and Dodgers in a virtual dead heat in the NL, both teams lost on the road, meaning that two summer-long pennant races had come down to the final day.

A pennant race can be a cruel mistress. I suppose that's what keeps bringing me back after all these years. Once you taste the electricity of a September spent on edge, you can hardly return to business as usual. Think of all the memories that have been made during our journey over the years, having never reached the destination. On this beautiful, sunny Opening Day morning, the Good Ship Mariner sets sail for one more such voyage. The horizon is empty, yet it's full of possibility. There are still memories left to be made. And when the day finally comes and we are hoisting our glasses to a World Series Champion, victory will taste that much sweeter after all the bitterness of Septembers past.

Who knows? Maybe that day is just around the corner.

On Sunday October 2, 1949, Duke Snider singled home Pee Wee Reese in the tenth inning on the final day of the National League season in Philadelphia, giving the Dodgers the NL pennant for the second time in three seasons. In New York, the Bronx Bombers took a 1-0 lead into the eighth inning when Tommy Henrich homered off of Red Sox great Mel Parnell, chasing him out of the game. The Yankees exploded for three more runs off of reliever Tex Hughson and won their sixteenth AL pennant. They went on to win the World Series in five games, leading Dodgers fans to groan, "Wait 'till next year."

Even in Brooklyn hope springs eternal.

2017: 78 WINS / 84 LOSSES

2018

Good Morning Friends:

On April 28, 1994 a woman by the name of Antwinica Bridgeman was found dead in the basement of her apartment building, the victim of a particularly brutal murder, even by the standards of a hardscrabble neighborhood like hers on the south side of Chicago. Bridgeman had disappeared seventeen days earlier after celebrating her twentieth birthday with some friends who lived in her building. The day prior to her disappearance, she had been seen with a man known to investigators only as "Chip." Police came to believe Chip was the brother of Bridgeman's upstairs neighbor. When witnesses verified that he was in attendance at Bridgeman's birthday celebration, he became the chief suspect.

The next day, the man who police believed to be Chip was arrested and interrogated by Chicago police officers. Nevest Coleman denied any involvement in the crime. In fact, he was quick to point out that he had been the one to discover the body and initially report Bridgeman's death to the authorities. After about a half hour of interrogation, though, a detective came into the room and punched Coleman twice in the head, telling him to answer their questions the "right" way. Coleman was told that he would be released if he implicated two other men in the murder of Bridgeman. The two other men were told the same thing and treated much the same way.

In May of 1997, despite no physical or forensic evidence linking him to the crime, and despite the fact that two of Coleman's colleagues testified as to his good character, Coleman was convicted of murder. He was ultimately fired from his job and sentenced to life in prison by a Cook County Circuit Court Judge. He served over twenty years in prison for a crime he didn't commit.

But he never lost hope.

In 2016, the Cook County "conviction integrity unit" began looking into Coleman's case. After the Illinois State Police crime lab reviewed clothing and fingernail clippings, DNA evidence excluded the three men charged with Bridgeman's murder from the profile of the actual attacker. The DNA was eventually matched to a serial rapist who lived not far from Bridgeman's apartment building. Last August, the Innocence Project filed a post-conviction petition to vacate the murder convictions based on the discovery of new evidence. The petition also included information about the detectives in Coleman's case, who had produced several false confessions in the intervening years. And although I would love nothing more than to exhaust every last detail of the case's procedural history, we do need to actually move on.

On December 1, 2017, the case against Nevest Coleman was dismissed after twenty three years. Despite the possibility of a potentially lucrative lawsuit against the police department awaiting him, and the fact that he hadn't eaten a home cooked meal in over two decades, when Coleman was released from prison he was asked about his first wish...

"To go back and work for the [Chicago] White Sox."

41

Before his incarceration, Coleman had worked as a grounds-keeper at the old Comiskey Park in Chicago.

Earlier this week, after twenty-four seasons without him, the White Sox welcomed Nevest Coleman back as a member of their grounds crew. The two colleagues who testified on his behalf at his trial, still working for the team, hugged Coleman when he walked into the new Comiskey park for the first time. Stepping into the sun-soaked ballpark and looking up at a brilliant blue sky must have been an amazing feeling for a man who had come to believe he would die in prison.

But hope never dies.

I must admit to feeling confined by a prison of my own these days, friends. We Mariner fans now suffer from the longest playoff drought in professional sports. And although I don't mean to make light of the actual harms suffered by the actual people in this very true story, we all know that I've done a lot worse over the years. Nevest Coleman's story is an illustration. Even when the hour is darkest, when there is every reason to give up, when the flame of hope has flickered down to mere ashes swirling through the smoke... after serving twenty three years of a life sentence... all it takes is that one fateful clerk to reach up on the shelf, blow the dust off your case file, and start reading...

Hope has to begin somewhere, Mariners fans. And maybe that day is today.

When Nevest Coleman was asked by a reporter after stepping back onto the baseball diamond for the first time,

42

"Mr. Coleman, what are you feeling right now?" Do you know what he said?

"Let's go win the pennant."

Hope springs eternal.

I am dedicating this year's message to Marty Lybecker. Marty was a family friend, a diehard Orioles fan, a staple recipient, and a frequent responder to this annual email, before he tragically passed away last summer. We exchanged many emails during the 2016 pennant race, when the Mariners and Orioles were dueling for a playoff berth. The last time I communicated with him was one year ago at this time, when he wrote me to say that [2017] would be the Mariners' year. He was always encouraging, generous, and a true student of baseball. RIP Marty.

2018: 89 WINS / 73 LOSSES

2019

Good morning friends!

Last season, as the summer reached a crescendo, our beloved Mariners built an apparently insurmountable lead in the American League wild card race. The spell which has seemingly bewitched the boys of summer since their record-setting 2001 season seemed to be breaking. There was joy in Mudville.... for a time. When the leaves began to fade, the hometown nine faded along with them, and the Good Ship Mariner succumbed to their Oakland rivals once again. Now, after our dalliance with the pennant race, the old ball club has undergone a "reimagining," and many of our heroes have departed for greener pastures. Some were traded to our bitter rivals. Even your veritable scribe cannot help but feel that we Mariner fans have entered the long night....

In the polar reaches of the world, once winter has truly set in, the sun trickles below the horizon, leaving nothing but frigid, bitter darkness for weeks at a time. No sunlight. Temperatures well below zero. Howling winds. Unforgiving storms. Mere survival in these conditions requires a deeply embedded constitution and character that few possess. And there is only one place where humans have been called upon to try....

In 1914, a group of investors set out to capture glory for the British Empire by financing an expedition to traverse the Antarctic continent. Veteran British polar explorer Ernest Shackleton was selected to command what came to be known as The Imperial Trans-Antarctic Expedition. Shackleton assembled a crew of twenty-eight men to sail to the edge of the world, make landfall and traverse the length of the Antarctic continent. It was the first mission of its kind. The men knew they would battle harrowing conditions. They expected to be gone for months in their quest to bring glory to the Empire. But dangerous seaward voyages, much like baseball seasons, do not always go according to plan....

On December 5, 1914 Shackleton and his men set sail from the tiny port of South Georgia, deep in the South Atlantic, toward the Antarctic coast aboard a ship known as *The Endurance*. His majesty's ship was built with a polar exploration such as this one in mind. She was meant not only to withstand the occasional collision with hefty icebergs, but to break through them and carve a path toward the Antarctic coast. *Endurance* was a sturdy 144-foot vessel, built with four layers of solid oak and Norwegian fir, measuring eighty-five inches thick at the bow, and weighing over one hundred-forty tons.

Shackleton knew something was amiss just two days into the journey when *Endurance* was forced to redirect around an unseasonably thick ice pack, still many miles from her destination. A week later, the ship became stuck between two ice floes for twenty-four hours until an oceanic shift broke it loose. This routine continued for many weeks, and *Endurance* was forced to merely drift among the icebergs at a snail's pace, traveling less than a mile per day. By the end of February, the expedition was badly behind schedule, and still miles from making landfall. Whispers began to circulate among the crew. The expedition might have to hunker down for the winter. March, April, and May passed. The ice was growing thicker and more unruly. The daylight hours waned. In June, the month-long night began....

No crew was more prepared for the challenge than this one. They had already proven they could survive for long stretches in frigid conditions. They used blubber oil to heat the cabins, and they were mostly protected from the elements inside the sturdy frame of *Endurance*. When the darkness ended in late June 1915, the crew was delighted to see the sun again, more hopeful than ever.

But what they heard on September 30, 1915 was the sound of devastation. *Endurance* had still not broken away from the thick ice pack, and now she was faced with her worst predicament yet: two large ice floes converged, enveloping the ship and lifting her up out of the water, tilting her to port. As the floes contracted, the crew could hear loud cracking in the hull. After weeks with no progress and the cracking getting worse, on October 24, another floe merged into the starboard side, and the quadruple-hull of *Endurance* was penetrated at last, giving way to a rush of icy water. Like the Good Ship Mariner, *The Endurance* was overtaken by an unruly sea.

Shackleton gave the order to abandon ship and ordered the lifeboats and any remaining provisions to be evacuated. The captain knew they were drifting in a northern direction, but his ability to pinpoint their exact location was imperfect. By Shackleton's rudimentary calculations, the nearest land was more than three hundred miles away. The men hiked westward across the drifting ice, but after three grueling days and barely two miles traveled carrying their lifeboats and a bounty of supplies, Shackleton ordered the men to make camp and wait for the ice to break up rather than try to haul the camp any further. For the next four months the men waited in the bitter coldness, using their lifeboats for shelter, hunting for seals and penguins. They feared they would not survive another winter.

It felt as though all hope was lost....

On April 8, 1916, the men were forced into action. The floe upon which they had been camping for over three months split apart, leaving the crew and most of their supplies on a relatively small, triangular sheet of ice floating amid the treacherous sea. It was now or never. Shackleton ordered the men to board the boats, take what provisions they could, and make for Elephant Island, which he now estimated to be just over a hundred miles away. The journey across the Antarctic ocean was perilous and miserable. The crew paddled with desperation for hours on end toward an empty horizon. Each wave that crashed into the boat was a lethal bath of ice water pouring over their bodies. Many men suffered frostbite in their extremities. Food was almost non-existent.

But they never stopped paddling....

After a week at sea, desperate of thirst and exhausted from days of furious rowing, the men spotted Elephant Island. It was a desolate place, with but few beaches suitable for making camp. There Shackleton made a brave and fateful decision. He would take five men and sail for South Georgia, eight hundred miles away. The rest of the men were ordered to wait on Elephant Island, their fate resting upon a twenty-two foot lifeboat, *The James Caird*. These men had been asked to sacrifice everything for the glory of the Empire. They had survived the long night, braved the most inhospitable conditions imaginable, eaten nothing but seal meat for months, and now they were being asked to endure another unruly winter.

Hope was their only choice....

48

As *The James Caird* sailed for South Georgia on April 24, the conditions were abysmal. Shackleton described the waves as being the largest he had ever seen in 26 years at sea. The navigation capabilities of the crew were crude, to be generous, at a time when precision was required. But a stiff northwesterly wind provided the team with the lucky break they needed, helping to guide *The James Caird* toward South Georgia. After fourteen long days, their rations depleted and ice accumulating in the bottom of the boat, Shackleton spotted land. When the men heard the Stromness steam whistle, they wept with joy. The South Georgian whalers had long since abandoned any thought of Shackleton's return. But despite insurmountable odds, truly hostile conditions, with only their cunning and determination to propel them, the Imperial Trans-Antarctic Expedition had survived the long night and nearly two years floating amidst the ice...

They never lost hope.

Each year at this time, I am reminded that spring is nature's promise of a new beginning. Once that first burst of warm sunlight breaks through winter's shield of gray clouds, it is easy to be seduced by the possibilities of the summer ahead. The Imperial Trans-Antarctic Expedition was seduced by possibilities of fame and glory. But rather than see their dreams realized, they were forced to endure a dark and hopeless winter. The long night. Their hope was reduced to a flicker. But the flame never went out. They lived to fight another day. And another. And another.

Just as the sun rises again after the long night, so too will our Mariners eventually rise in the American League West. As we begin the journey again today, the Good Ship Mariner is stocked with supplies, the crew is rested and ready to emerge from its winter hibernation. The sails are at full mast. A glorious victory is just beyond the horizon. We cannot see it, but we know it is there. We hope we will reach it this year, maybe it will be next. But we must always hope....

We have no other choice....

Hope springs eternal.

2019: ?

Alex Tuttle is a Pacific Northwest native and baseball enthusiast, a tragic combination that has resulted in him becoming a lifelong Mariners fan. The first baseball game Alex attended had the misfortune of being played in the Kingdome, in 1988 (the Mariners lost to the Twins). Although Alex was a skilled catcher in his youth, he couldn't hit a lick, and his dreams of playing professional baseball were dashed when he didn't make the eighth grade summer all-star team. Alex lives in Seattle, Washington with his wife, Martha. During his free time, he serves as his fantasy baseball league commissioner.